LIFE

IT'S NOT SUPPOSED TO BE LIKE THIS

EMMITT MCKENZIE

ISBN: 979-8986943862
PB

This book is dedicated to anyone who has struggled with sexual abuse, alcohol, drug use, gang life, single-parenting homes, and anything else that constantly reminds you that LIFE Isn't Supposed to Be Like This.

TABLE OF CONTENTS

FOREWORD

Emmitt McKenzie shares his life story with all the passion, pain, and redemption with which he lives his life. You must read this story and see the amazing grace of Jesus Christ lived out in difficult circumstances. You will be moved by this story. But most of all you will be motivated to follow Christ with even more passion and appreciation for what God can do. This book will remind us that the Lord Jesus saves, restores, and blesses all those who will turn to Him in repentance. Emmitt travels the nation sharing the story of Christ's saving power and now, by reading this book, you can experience that amazing grace of Jesus Christ for yourself.

—Michael Spradlin, Ph.D., President
Mid-America Baptist Theological Seminary
The College at Mid-America

CHAPTER 1

VIOLENCE AND FEAR

I can't even remember all the places I lived in as a child. While they were all different; somehow, they were all the same. Low income, small places; some houses some apartments that were built out of desperation to house the growing population of Oklahoma City. Even as a child, I knew these places were too small for our family. Most of the homes we lived in were beyond disrepair, often as abused and neglected as the residents inside. One reason I have trouble remembering all the different places we lived is because we moved around a lot. We never moved far distances, in fact until recently, I had never really been out of the state of Oklahoma, but I have lived in more homes than I can count. However, the main reason I can't remember all the different houses is due to the years I spent abusing drugs to try to forget all the fear and violence of my childhood that took place in those neglected houses.

I came into the world as Emmitt Richard Lee McKenzie, my mother and father had recently married and moved in with my father's parents. My parents were only trying to provide a life for their family, but they were not off to a fair start. Both of my parents only knew a life entangled in alcohol abuse, violence, and fear. Before they met, my mom was single parent to my older sister; and she was living with her parents and going to school in Anadarko, Oklahoma. My dad was also living and going to school in Anadarko and his parents only lived a block from my mom's parents. This was convenient because they didn't have a place to live after they got married. So, they moved in with my dad's parents, yet the alcohol abuse would fuel fights that would cause my mom to go stay at her parent's house. From the beginning of my life, I was being moved around to escape the violence and fear, but it always found me.

My mom's mother, Grandma Juanita, played an important role in my mom's life raising her oldest child and despite struggling with her own alcoholism she became a stable environment for my older sister, who ended up living with my Grandma Juanita most of my childhood. My dad's mom, Grandma Joanne, became my stability in childhood. Grandma Joanne loved me, but the drinking and violence around her house are still fresh in my mind. I was the first-born grandchild, and we spent a lot of time together. On Sunday mornings, she would take me to church and that is where I first heard the name of Jesus in the song, "Jesus loves me". Grandma Joanne would often tell me she thought I would grow up to be a pastor, but I never believed her.

My parent's continued to live with my dad's parents in Anadarko, and they had two more kids during this time, my younger sister and brother. Looking back, I can see that everyone involved in my family, was trying to do the best they could with what little they had, but the emotional and physical abuse was a family legacy. As a child, I witnessed so much fear and violence at the hands of my family. Most of the violence came directly from the long days of drinking on the weekends at my Grandma Joanne's house. Family and friends would gather at her house, to drink and eat throughout the weekend.

On one hand my Grandma Joanne was a source of light and love, but on the other hand, I was also introduced to a lot of fear and violence at her house. Fear and violence in the form of alcoholism and abuse that stemmed from my grandpa and his friends drinking all day on the weekends. The same weekends that would end with my grandma taking me to church and the whole family would gather around the dining table, my dad, aunts, and uncles. They would bless the food and then open another bottle of whatever liquor was the cheapest that weekend. At the table, we were a pleasant family, but dinner would end, and the drinking would consume every adult in my family. I would watch as the adults in my family fought. Arguments fueled by liquor, often escalating beyond words into a brawl.

It is not supposed to be like this, life that is. As far back as I can remember I knew there had to be something different, something better in life. I couldn't understand then what I understand now. Today, I understand that God never intended for life to be full of violence and fear here on earth. As I reflect on my life for this book, I realize how thankful I am to have the opportunity to share my story. A story of a real person; raised with an absent father, an alcoholic mother, and who was sexually abused. I experienced gut wrenching violence and fear by the time I was a toddler. It wasn't a fear of being burned or fear of heights, but that of violence. The scariest forms of violence are rooted in humanity. The pains that humans can inflict from one person to another has the ability to stop you far short of seeing your destiny become your present.

In an attempt to run away from the pain in Anadarko, my family moved to Oklahoma City. My dad worked as a roofer, and we lived next door to the roofing company that hired him. One day, while my dad was at work, my mother was studying for her G.E.D. at the tiny square table in the small makeshift dining room that was connected to the cramped kitchen in our house. She was multitasking, trying to study while she cooked dinner. She had started a pot of water and potatoes on the stove in preparation for an economical dinner. Trying to not disrupt my mom's studies, my siblings and I decided to play "fast food drive-thru" with the oven door open. We were using the open oven as a drive-thru window. At the beginning we would take turns speaking into the oven giving our food orders. As time passed, we got impatient and we all, myself, my sister, and my brother began to lean on the oven door and our combined weight tipped the stove over on us. I pushed my brother and sister out of the way because I remembered the pot of boiling water and potatoes that was cooking on the top of the stove. They were safe, but I was stuck under the stove as the scorching water and potatoes splashed on my back. Trapped under the weight of the stove, I began to panic. I was screaming at the top of my lungs knowing that I should be in excruciating pain, but I felt nothing. Maybe I was in shock but looking back I think I was screaming because my mom was screaming. The tension inside the house was thick as everyone is the house feared the out-come. Frantically, my mother freed me from being under the oven, carried me to the bathroom sink and began to take my leather belt off. I could feel the belt shrinking from the hot water. Once free from the belt, she began to care-fully remove my clothes. However, the searing water had melted my skin and clothes together. My skin peeled off as my mom removed each layer of my clothes. My mom, with my siblings, rushed me to Children's Hospital 5 miles away. I had third degree burns on my back that required a 5X5 inch skin graft to repair. They took the graft from my right thigh, which was equally as painful as the burn. I ignored the doctors' instructions to sleep on my back and the graft got stuck to the sheet of the hospital bed. It took 3 months of recovery in the hospital and most days I was all alone. My mom couldn't visit very often because she didn't have childcare for my siblings. Occasionally, my family would visit in the evenings after my dad got off work. It was a short visit that was never long enough, and every time they left, I would be angry and begin to cry. My only comfort was through a little ministry at the hospital that provided stuffed animals for kids in recovery. I would cling to the stuff animal until I had cried myself to sleep. The physical pain was manageable, but the emotional pain would haunt me for the rest of my childhood. I wanted to go home; little did I know that my home was going to crumble in a short amount of time.

After I returned home, the fighting that we thought

we had escaped when we moved to OKC returned. I was happy to be home after the incident, but my dad blamed my mom for the accident. I was used to seeing this cycle of love and hate ever since my grandma's house, but it hurt more watching it happen to my family after being away from them for so long. Eventually, I would see my dad less and less as he would leave for work and not come home until after I was asleep. It progressed to where I didn't see him but one time a week. Finally, he left for work one day and never came back. I was left asking myself, "Do my parents even love me if they can't love each other?" This was just the beginning of my pains with fear and violence as God worked out my very own creation story.

"For we know that the whole creation
groans and labors with birth-pangs
together until now." Romans 8:22

CHAPTER 2

ABANDONED

G rowing up in Oklahoma, I was no stranger to violent storms. I have watched storms on the far-off horizon build until the storm sweeps across towns and cities with force and violence that leave the landscape changed forever. My life was a violent storm. I would watch the dark clouds form across the horizon of my family, my parent's drinking until their minds were clouded with darkness and evil. The distant rumblings of thunder would start of soft and build until the thunder of hurtful words and actuations would rattle the windows of our house. The lightening of sharp quick physical abuse would flash and fill the whole house leaving me and my siblings breathless. Often with a storm, you run to a corner and curl up as small as you can praying for the violence of the storm to stop. Surviving a violent storm is no different than surviving an abusive family life. I have hidden in the smallest corner of my different houses with my sibling waiting for the violence and abuse of the drunk storms of my parents to end. Almost every problem we had in our family could be solved with alcohol and violence. Even though my parents were separated, it did not bring relief from the violence and fear in my life. Unfortunately, my dad still had things at the house, and he would show up here and there to get his stuff. A few times my mother's new boyfriend would be visiting when my dad would come to get his stuff and he would get jealous. One time, I watched my dad being chased with a twelve-inch military style knife by my mother's boyfriend. My siblings and I were terrified by these encounters often fearing for our lives waiting for the storm to pass. I remember we would all go into my bedroom and hide in a corner screaming until we were out of breath, or the conflict was over. These kinds of meetings carried on for a while and eventually my dad wanted to keep me or as I remember, my mother's boyfriend didn't like me. In that moment, I felt like no one wanted me like I had been abandoned by everyone in my life continuing the feelings of being alone that started in the hospital.

After I moved in with my dad, his girlfriend began to abuse me while he was at work. She was a young mother with 4 kids of her own and taking on a troubled fifth child was more than she could handle. I would get in trouble for everything and her go-to punishment was to put dish soap in my mouth and sit me next to the hot furnace on my knees for what seemed like an hour. The dish soap was thick, and the chemical taste would mix with my spit until I couldn't stand it anymore and I would spew it out into the furnace. In the winter, the furnace would turn on and I would have to sit there as the air got warmer and warmer until I could hardly breathe. She was always right beside me ready to fill my mouth again or make sure I didn't move away from the heat; and from my perspective as a child, she was as close as you could get to a wicked witch. Her daughter was two years older than me, her son my age, and she had two toddlers. The boy my age always picked fights with me. The solution my dad and stepmom came up with was to have us fight each other in front of them.

I quickly learned that fighting was the only way to resolve any conflicts. The one who lost got hit with the belt. Often times after fighting with my stepbrother, I would long to be with my mother and siblings, even though life wasn't perfect with them either it was better than all the physical fighting and abuse I was experiencing living with my dad. But most of all, I missed my grandma, she was the only source of love in my life. One night, I woke up crying for my grandma and went downstairs to my dad. Annoyed by my crying and more than likely drunk, he hit me with the belt and told me to shut up. In that moment, I knew something was wrong and I could not shake that feeling for the next few days. My dad was withholding from me that my grandma was very sick, and she ended up passing away a few days later. The funeral was the scariest thing I had ever encountered up to that point in my life, I had not been confronted with death and the feeling of losing the one source of love intensified my feelings of abandonment. I still remember the song "Amazing Grace" played at the funeral and now every time I hear it, I think of my grandma. Before I became a Christian, I found comfort from fear in remembering all the times she rocked me to sleep by singing to me. I believe the reason she was my refuge from the violence in my life was because of the light of Christ in her.

After my grandma died, my life continued to be unstable, going between my Aunt Jinny's and my dad's house. My dad was not taking my grandma's death well which amplified his alcohol use which in turn led to more abusive behavior. It was typical that my dad and his girlfriend would go out for the night and leave his girlfriend's oldest daughter in charge. Her routine was to put the smaller children to be bed early and then try to stay up until our parents made it home. This gave her time to do things that she knew her mother would not approve of like smoking cigarettes. One night, she started to pressure me to join her in smoking a cigarette in a closet. In that moment, I knew it was wrong to go with her. However, I was faced with violence again, either from her or my dad. She threatened to beat me up if I didn't join her. I was also sure that more violence would come if my dad ever found out the truth.

To avoid the immediate threat of violence, I went to the closet with her, and we sat in the darkness smoking.

This was my first experience smoking and with each inhale I felt the rush of the nicotine fill my body. I became more relaxed until we both heard a car door shut. Our relaxed bodies snapped to attention as we were certain our parents had come home early. In a rush to get rid of the evidence, she threw the lit cigarette into the little attic trap door, and it came to rest on top of the insulation in the roof. She ran downstairs to talk to her mom, while I pretended to be asleep next to the toddlers who were two and three years old at that time. Our parents ended up leaving again and we tried to stay up waiting for them, but we fell asleep. In the middle of the night, I woke up and the whole room was filled with white smoke. I couldn't see, I couldn't breathe, and the temperature was rising inside the bedroom. I tried walking to the door to go downstairs but ended up tripping on the two little ones. I pulled myself up off the floor, felt my way along the hot walls, and finally made it to the door. I ran downstairs to my dad's room to wake them. I started to yell about the fire upstairs, but they were wasted, and nothing would rouse them. With moments to spare, they woke up just in time to get everyone out of the house.

First responders started to show up; helplessly all we could do was sit on the curb and watch the house burn to the ground. Like the house consumed with flames, I too was consumed the flames confusion, fear, and devastation. So, when the daughter started to accuse me of smoking in the house and causing the fire, I was caught off guard. After the first responders examined us and the police took a statement, my dad loaded me up and took me a few blocks down the road to my Aunt Jinny's house. He took me into a room with his belt, grabbed me by the hand, and began to beat me while swinging me around in a circle. My back and bottom had whelps on them for days and I couldn't sit down. After my dad left, my aunt asked me what happened, and I told her everything. I was physically hurt but the emotional pain of my dad not believing me was harder to bear. In that moment, I learned to take responsibility for things I didn't do. As life continued to progress, I knew that just surviving was not the way life was meant to be.

After my dad accused me of starting the fire, he no longer wanted to take responsibility for me. So, I moved in with Aunt Jinny. She enrolled me into the school across the street, Columbus Elementary. It was nice since my cousin also attended school there. My mom would pick me up and keep me on the weekends and I could visit my siblings. My dad would come visit me sometimes, but not very often. He moved in with his girlfriend's mother and conveniently had no room for me. My dad took the easy way out most of the time. I remember the last time I had an interaction with him, he promised to take my siblings and I to the Oklahoma State Fair. We waited all day and night, but he never showed. I guess he took his retirement money, and moved to Denver, Colorado with his girlfriend. My education on empty promises and abandonment was complete.

In my aunt's house, the same cycle of stress, alcoholism, and abuse continued. Eventually, my aunt sent me to live with one of my other aunts in Anadarko. I was shuffled around living with my aunts and uncles not knowing what was coming next, all the while feeling more and more alone. Nothing was stable and alcoholism was prevalent in every home. I was able to spend a lot of time with my cousins, whom I love, but being the first-born grandchild came with responsibilities and privileges. The way my aunts and uncles loved me and took care of me stirred jealousy with my cousins. They would tell me to go home to my own mom and dad, saying, "your mom and dad don't love you," or other harsh things that made me feel unwanted and abandoned. When I felt like nobody loved me, I would miss Grandma Joanne and would cry myself to sleep longing for her to rock me to sleep so I could feel loved again. Eventually, Aunt Jinny took me back in and I moved back to Oklahoma City. I was a child, yet the world was revealing itself to me, this world full of fear, violence, and abandonment. Deep down in my heart, I knew there was more to life. I would think back on the song from my childhood, "Jesus loves me this I know, for the Bible tells me so little ones to him belong, they are weak, but He is strong. YES, Jesus loves me…".

> *"I will love you, O Lord, my strength. The LORD is my rock and my fortress and my deliverer; my God, my strength, in whom I trust; My shield and the horn of my salvation, my stronghold. "Psalm 18:1-2*

CHAPTER 3

SEXUALLY ABUSED (BEYOND FEAR)

Once I had settled back into Aunt Jinny's house, my mother had bumped into my aunt at a laundry mat in OKC. When my Aunt Jinny told me that she had run into my mom I remember thinking that I hardly remembered what my mom looked like. At that point, my mom took me back into her home and it felt good to be wanted. It might be hard to keep track of all the homes, but that is exactly the point. I was being passed around all my childhood with very little thought to my well-being. This time I found joy being with my siblings, it was comforting and familiar despite the drinking and violence that continued every day at the hand of my mom's boyfriend. There were good days and those are the days that gave me hope and made me wonder why it couldn't be normal every day. I weighed my circumstances and began to think about all the places I had lived. Desperately, I was trying to remember any piece of love I might have encountered. The truth is, I knew there was something better in life and it wasn't in any of the places I had been. I love everyone who took care of me, but fear conquered my childhood. However, I was about to find out there was a place beyond fear.

I cannot remember the reason we were going to visit my Grandpa Richard and Grandma Juanita in Anadarko, but I do remember that my mother was drinking and driving on our way there. A cop pulled the car over and my mom was arrested in Chickasha, Oklahoma. I watched as the police officer took my mom away in handcuffs and me and my siblings were taken away in a different car to a DHS Facility in Chickasha. I was scared. We were in an unfamiliar town, and I felt responsible for my younger siblings. At the DHS facility, they separated me and my brother from my sister. We had to stay there for two nights until they transferred us from Chickasha to Anadarko. My older sister Renea who lived with Grandma Juanita and Grandpa Richard for as long as I could remember came to visit us in the Anadarko DHS facility. She told us that she loved us and encouraged us to take care of each other. But I couldn't understand why we couldn't stay with her and my grandparents at their house until my mom was released from jail. I felt abandoned again. With no relatives willing to take in my brother and sister and I, we went into foster care. They sent me and my brother Joe to one foster home and sent my younger sister Tosha to different home.

The foster home we stayed at was only for a couple of months, but it left a big impression on me. It was the first time I remember decorating a tree for Christmas. The family had a tradition of stringing popcorn together to hang on the tree, I thought it was forced child labor since I had never experienced anything like that before. The next foster home we stayed at was out in the country. Far away from anything I was familiar with, the house sat on a dirt road and there were cattle in the fields next to the house. There was a pond near the house that I would go to and skip rocks as I thought about all the friends I had left behind in the city. Even though I was with my brother, Joe, and the family had two boys, I felt alone. In the city, I could walk outside my door and be surrounded by all my neighborhood friends. Here in the foster home, there was no one else around for miles. We had to travel 3 miles back into town to go to school and the only image I can remember from the school is the basketball court. It was hard for me to make friends at school, I had nothing in common with the other kids. I had never experienced farm life. I remember the foster family took us on a trip to watch sheep getting sheered. I never knew much about animals, but I thought it was awesome to see what my clothes were made of.

The family seemed like nice people to live with; especially without the presence of alcohol, yet I wasn't fully happy. Can someone ever be happy in the situation I was in? Other than missing my family, the place was a stable environment compared to what I had been in. I found out what structure was in a home; we had to go to bed at a certain time, we ate at a certain time, and we woke up at a certain time. The foster family had a boy around Joe's age and an older high school boy who was a local basketball hero. We would spend many nights watching him play basketball at the school gym. Joe, the younger boy, and I shared a room and the older boy slept downstairs in a finished basement. The basement door was in the center of the house and the stairs down into the basement were carpeted and had a ramp down the side that we used as a slide. I thought the basement was the coolest place in the whole house. Since the basement was the room for the oldest boy, we were not allowed to play on the stairs or in the basement very often.

The basement became the scene of my worst nightmare. One night, I was able to spend the night downstairs. There was only one huge bed downstairs that we, the high school kid and I both slept on that night. I remember falling asleep and in the middle of the night he took my pants and underwear off of me. It was then that he sodomized me. I didn't know what to do! He was a big guy, and I couldn't fight him off. I never told anyone, and I wish I had. I was just a kid, but I knew what he did to me was wrong. I carried on with life as normal as I could. Even though it only happened one time, it still haunts me to this day. No child should ever have to experience that evil. As time passed; I grew angry at everyone in my life who caused me to be in that foster home in the first place. I felt more abandoned than ever. It felt like no one cared about me and the things that I was going through. How could the people in my life love me and let all this evil happen to me?

I praise God we didn't stay much longer in that house. My mother eventually gained custody of us once again. I never told anyone about that night in the basement until I confided in a girlfriend when I was a teenager and then I finally confronted it when I was 31, while in a treatment facility. The years of keeping it bottled up inside, damaged me. I wish I would have spoken-up because the high school boy should have been taught the responsibility of his actions to protect others in the future. I wish I had told someone. I was just a kid and I know now it never should have happened. I became angry, embarrassed, and ashamed which led to me acting out.

> *"But as for you, you meant evil against*
> *me; but God meant it for good, in order*
> *to bring it about as it is this day, to save*
> *many people alive." Genesis 50:20*

CHAPTER 4

BEHAVIOR PROBLEMS

There was a constant storm in my life. Dark clouds, thunderous ringing, bright flashes of confusion; I was surrounded by chaos. Living with my mom again meant I was trapped in the cycle of stress, alcoholism, and abuse. I was beginning to internalize the darkness and it forced its way out in harmful behaviors. If there was a conflict with another kids, all I knew to do was fight them. Violence was the answer to every problem. However, there were moments, little glimmers, where I could feel the love of Christ in my life like I had when I was with my grandma. One constant glimmer of hope in my life was the bus ministries of the Baptist churches in the different neighbors we lived. No matter where we moved there was a church member knocking on our door asking if we would like a ride to church. I liked going to church and I heard the Gospel. In fact, I liked it so much I can recall walking the aisle and "getting saved" three times at three different churches. I didn't understand the importance of repentance. It just felt good to think I was saved from all the evil I had encountered in my life. Church also reminded me of my grandma, and I naively thought that going to church meant you went to heaven. I wanted to be with my grandma more than anything else and if church was a way to do that then I was going to church. I didn't want to be on this cursed earth any longer because the world continued to show its ugly face to me. All the evil that I had encountered in my life, all because of the sin other people, had driven me to a place that led me to act out.

While living with my mom, we were all over the city because she moved all the time. We were never in a house for more than a year. During this time, I went to five different elementary schools. There was no stability. I can remember living in a small brown duplex. A neighborhood friend and I had built a bike ramp one day and enjoyed riding our bikes off the ramp feeling like we were BMX stars. Also living in the neighborhood was an 18-year-old boy who thought it made him cool to bully us. He would make jokes about us and laugh at us. One day, we went into my house after playing with the ramp to eat lunch with my siblings while my mother was at work. If I had to guess, we were enjoying one of our favorite meals, raw Ramen noodles with the seasoning pack. While were sitting around the table, we began to hear a loud banging noise from outside. We looked out the window to witness the 18-year-old boy destroying our ramp with a sledgehammer all the while laughing. Rage filled my entire body, and the next thing I knew I had my BB gun in my hand pumping it for max force. I took aim out the window and hit the 18-year-old in the finger. Furious, he took off towards my back door. I tried to beat him to the backdoor before he could enter our house, but I was too late. He kicked the back door open, charged toward me, and kicked me in the stomach. Listen, I tried my best to be a good kid most of the time, despite all I had been through I made good grades in school, and I tried to get along with everyone, but when he destroyed the bike ramp, something inside me snapped. I know I should not have shot him; I just could not stand silently while this guy bullied us. In the end neither one of us was right in the eyes of God.

The next few years were all the same, different versions of my mom being abused by her boyfriends and moving us to a different house to escape the abuse. One time, her boyfriend beat her with a baseball bat. He had chased my mother to the front yard, and they were both screaming at each other. I went outside to see what was going on and that is when the police arrived. One of the neighbors had witnessed the fight and called the police. The police arrested the boyfriend, but not before he inflicted some serious bruising to my mother. After he got out of jail, my mother stayed with him. My mother would try to escape her own reality by going to her friend's house to party and most of the time she would force us to go with her.

Finally, we moved back to Southeast OKC to the 3-block neighborhood I fondly remember because of the friendships I had made. Our house sat up a steep driveway, and my new best friend, Tommy, lived down the street. We would play football in the middle of the street with other neighborhood friends. I enjoyed time away from home because my siblings and I would fight all the time. One day, one of my football buddies came to visit me on his bike and I went to the street to talk to him. He had brought a bag of candy with him that he shared with me and we sat there talking for a little while. Candy was rare in my house, and it was a treat that he was sharing his with me. My brother, Joe, made his way to us from the front porch and asked for some candy but the kid refused to share with him. Jealous of the candy and furious that he wouldn't share with him, Joe stormed off into the house slamming the screen door behind him. We hear the door slam again and we see Joe standing on the front porch with a steak knife in his hand. From the porch, he threw the knife and hit the kid right between the temple and eye. The kid reached up to his eye and blood started to gush out as the knife fell to the ground. He left his bike, ran down the street to his house and soon first responders began to fill our street.

At the time of the knife incident, my mom worked during the day at a hotel cleaning rooms. We didn't have much but her job took care of us. I was never hungry and was content with what we had but our situation changed after my brother hurt that kid with the knife. My mother had had enough, and she was struggling to deal with both my brother's and I's behavioral problems. Now, my mother was overwhelmed and wanted to send us away. We had lived in this house for 2 years; I did not want to leave my friends and the little bit of stability that was beginning to be established. However, my brother and I were a powder keg primed to explode with destructive behavior.

My mother put us in the Baptist Boys Home. They almost didn't take us because there was a certain age requirement, and my brother was a year too young. He ended up being the youngest child on the grounds. There were all types of boys at the Baptist Boys Home ranch; boys abandoned by their parents, boys with behavior issues, or boys with issues with law enforcement. Eight boys lived in our cottage and a live-in family took care of us. All together there were about five cottages and ours was the smallest on the ranch. We were required to do chores and mow the grass; it was a huge place. Mowing grass made me feel like a man, I was working but wasn't getting paid. It inspired me to be a man. At the age of 9 and 10 years old, toys were no longer my thing and working became something I enjoyed.

There were programs we were required to get involved in and we would train and take care of livestock. I eventually got involved with the horses and swine at separate times while on the ranch. In my first rodeo, I rode on a pony carrying the American flag and competed in a barrel race on the same pony. Another time, I chose a piglet as it grew I trained the pig for livestock shows. Eventually, they took me to show it at the state fair grounds. I learned to do many things at the boy's home, and I really appreciated the structure. There was never a dull moment and many things to do like swimming after we had done all our chores. However, swimming depended on if we got into trouble or not. I used to lay on the sidewalk at night looking at the stars. The first time I saw a shooting star, I jumped up, ran inside and told the cottage parents. They just smiled. The shooting star sparked a thought within me and I began to think about the cosmos God had made.

Fifth grade quickly came, and I continued to be a good

kid at school and make good grades. The teachers always liked me, maybe it was because they felt sorry for me. They knew that I was living at the ranch. Teachers in the area were familiar with the ranch and knew something dramatic had happened in order for me to be living out there. Every Sunday we went to Waterloo Baptist Church in Guthrie, and I continued to hear the gospel. I enjoyed church and it was a place where I felt peace and love by the people of God. We would sing out of the Baptist Hymnal, and I learned those great songs of theology. On Sunday mornings we went to Sunday school, then to Children's Church, and on Wednesday evenings we sat with the adults in "big church". For a time, the cycle of stress, alcoholism, and violence were absent from my life.

"So shall My word that goes forth from
My mouth; It shall not return to Me void,
but it shall accomplish what I please and it
shall prosper in the thing for which I sent
it." Isaiah 55:11

CHAPTER 5

NOMAD TO WEASEL

My family had been suffering for generations with alcoholism. In fact, my mother lived with her grandparents when she was growing up because of her parent's alcoholism. Proof that my sister living with my mother's parents was a sort of family legacy. My mother had a strong relationship with her grandma Clara, whom she shares a name. When grandma Clara was diagnosed with Alzheimer's and put in a nursing home in Tahlequah; my mother checked us out of the Baptist Boys Home and moved us all to Tahlequah to take care of her. I used to visit my grandmother every day at the nursing home. While in Tahlequah, I found a church down the street near our new house. It happened to be the Baptist church that minis-tered at the same nursing home my grandma was in. The church would have students put together care packages to send to the residences, and on Christmas Eve we went caroling at the nursing home. I enjoyed it because I was able to sing to my great grandmother about Jesus' birth.

While in Tahlequah, my mother started to date a new guy and like most of the guys my mother dated, he was abusive especially when he was drunk. It was normal for my mother to wake us up in the middle of the night after she was beat by her boyfriends. We would tip toe around to escape the abuse while her boyfriend would be passed out drunk. It was normal for us to miss a week of school as we avoided her boyfriends and tried to find a new place to start over. This time, my mother decided it was best for us to not return to Tahlequah. This guy was very violent, and it scared my mother. He eventually found us. However, my mother had rekindled an old relationship with the boyfriend she had before she left OKC. Once the boyfriend from Tahlequah realized that my mother had moved on it did not end well. One of the boyfriends stabbed the other one with a military style knife right in front of me. I thought I had witnessed someone get killed. He was lifeless on the ground, and it scared me to think he was gone forever. Miraculously he survived even after both lungs were punctured.

During this time, my older sister had moved in with us and we began to get drunk in the middle of the night while my mom was already lit. The neighbors would buy the beer for us, this also included my friend Brandon as he would buy the beer when he had extra lunch money saved up. Eventually, my mom found beer cans under our beds, and she sat us down to talk about the drinking. I thought we were in big trouble, so we argued that the reason we were drinking was because of all the horrible things we been through so far in our short lives. She broke down with tears filling her eyes as she grieved over her parenting up to that point in our lives. She blamed herself for our alcohol use. Instead of dealing with the family trauma and issues; we started drinking together as a family. I was 13 years old and learned to deal with trauma by abusing alcohol.

We eventually moved back to the area close to the school I attended before we went to the Baptist Boys

Home. The area was 3 square blocks of low-income housing that had a hold on me, it would draw me back into its borders time and time again. I caught up with some of the old friends that I used played football in the street with a few years back. We were older now, and we spent our time hanging out, listening to music, and drinking. We would spend hour listening to all the rappers of the late 80's and early 90's. Those rap songs were real to me. I was living the rhymes the rapper's spit.

Influenced by all the rap music, me and my friends decided to form a clique. There was only five of us, but we had watched enough movies and music videos to know that part of creating a clique meant that we had to fight each other. Since most my friends had lived in the neighborhood most of their lives and I had not, I was the only one they jumped into the clique by fighting. I took on two of my friends to prove my loyalty to them. I felt accepted for the first time in my life and the feelings of abandonment were fading away. We would skip school so we could have more time to learn the business of selling weed. Earning money was becoming my only focus, I thought it would make my life better.

During this time, I earned my street name, me and my clique were out late one night trying to rob unlocked cars. I was told to keep a look out for approaching cars and whistle if I saw anything. I opened the car door to hide behind it, sweating with the anticipation of getting caught. I knew it would be my fault if we got caught so I was making every effort to watch for cops. Frequently, I would jump up on the door frame to get some height to look over the roof of the car. Keeping my head on a swivel so I wouldn't make any mistakes. I was proud of my efforts. Finally, we were all back in the car with hearts racing from adrenaline. The oldest member through a joint into my lap and said, "Light that up, Weasel. He christened me with the street name weasel because he said I looked like a weasel popping up out of their holes in the earth looking around for incoming danger.

My family continued to move around the Southside of OKC and I had been to at least five different middle and junior high schools. I eventually ended up at Del City High School, where I was kicked out for smoking weed. I tried to enroll in the roughest school in south OKC, but they refused to take me in and stated that they didn't want my kind at their school. My clique was my stability during this time, but as we entered high school even my clique was getting smaller. I watched as each one of my homies joined a gang. I was the last one to join the gang. I began to kick out the screen of my bedroom window to sneak out to hang out with my friends and their new gang. I needed to prove that I had heart and was willing to fight for this gang and not punk out. One night at a party, my clique introduced me to the gang leaders. The leaders looked me up and down, then said, "What hood are you from?" Without missing a beat, I responded with their gang. As soon as the words left my mouth, five guys surrounded me on all sides. It was dark and I was drunk; punches started coming from every direction. The first punch hit me in the face, and I fell to the ground. My heart was beating loud inside my chest and my brain was telling me to stand up. I couldn't punk out now, every time they knocked me to the ground I stood up. Finally, the last punch was thrown, and I was officially a gang member. I woke up the next morning and took inventory of the damage. I had a black eye, busted lip, and the side of my head was swollen. All I told my mom was that I got in a fight, but soon she would find out I was part of a gang. Gang life had taken over my mentality, so much so that I knew I was going to die in the Southeast side of OKC. I would hardly venture out of the Southeast radius of the hood. Gang life all over America had blown up. It seemed like every day you could die for a bigger cause than yourself and I was willing to take the risk because I didn't have anything worth saving.

We moved inside of a neighborhood that was controlled by another gang and it was there my homeboys, and I made and even bigger name for ourselves. Our gang originally came out of the Northwest side of the city, but we were growing in numbers and so was our reputation. Not to mention the quantity and quality of drugs that we were moving and the number of guns we possessed. I had about eight different handguns under my bed along with a shotgun. I felt like I was living in a movie just like all those rappers talked about in their songs. The love of money brought respect, drugs, alcohol, and women into my life. Being a part of a gang gave me the false sense of a powerful life at the age of 16. I went to live with my best friend Tommy, who I used to play football with, in the streets. He went to the same school his whole life and I moved from school to school, but we ended up in the same gang. We became close and through the years our friendship grew into a brotherhood.

Tommy and I spent a lot of time together and on occasion I would ask him to give me a ride to church. I knew I was living in sin, but I wasn't ready to give up the gang lifestyle. The Holy Spirit would convict me, but I knew I was not going to stop. I would hear the preacher preach and I would be moved to tears knowing that I committed sins against God. But over and over I rejected the grace that was given to me because I wanted to do what I wanted; I was unwilling to repent. Repent means "to change the direction of life you are living into a new direction of following Christ". Brother Mike, who was the deacon of the church, would often come pick me up to take me to church. One time at my mom's house, Brother Mike pulled up in the church van just as I had finished selling drugs to someone in a car. I took a drink of my beer and as I turned around, he looked right at me and asked if I wanted to go to church. I tried to hide the beer and drop it behind me, but I knew he had seen me drinking. I was embarrassed, but he never scolded me about the beer instead, he showed me grace and love by still inviting me to church. I was slowly detaching from church and Brother Mike watched as I slipped away. I look back now and see how important he was to my life. I am grateful for the gospel seeds he planted.

Tommy would pick me up after church and we would immediately begin hustling as if we never skipped a beat. I had no real intention of changing my behavior. In fact, on more than one occasion, I would go to church high. The preachers voice would thunder in my ears, and I would hallucinate that it was God talking to me. We partied a lot and I started using cocaine. In one week, the police pulled us over every day, and I ended up going to a juvenile holding facility for possession of cocaine, a gun, and multiple marijuana charges. I was also arrested for breaking into a store after hours trying to get beer. The first time I got away, but the second time the case of beers broke and left a trail of beer that led the cops directly to my house. They arrested and charged me with Second Degree Burglary to a Business.

"For the love of money is a root of all kinds
of evil, for which some have strayed from
the faith in their greediness and pierced
themselves through many sorrows."
II Timothy 6:10

CHAPTER 6

NO HOPE

I was 16 years old when my mother put me in counseling once a week. She could see my depression. It was visible for anyone to see; my main coping skill was to bang my head against walls and other hard surfaces. A psychiatrist diagnosed me with manic depression to be treated with Zoloft and Trazadone. I would take Zoloft for the depression and the Trazadone helped me sleep at night. On the side, I mixed this medicine with the drugs and alcohol that I was already taking. My mother couldn't figure out why out of nowhere I would sit and cry before she took me to counseling. To be honest, I was reflecting on the sixteen years of my life and wondered why I had to be the one to live it. It was a horribly traumatic life. I wondered why I was even born, and I would cry at the fact I was sexually abused. The drugs and alcohol would offer temporarily relief to the shame I felt, but they would wear off and the shame was still there. It made me angry, and that is why I hit my head on walls, many times until I bled. I wanted to forget my past.

Hanging out with my homies I never dared mention it to any of them because I was embarrassed. My manhood, or what I thought was my manhood at the time, had been taken from me. I couldn't let my pride, the image that I had built get exposed to the jokes of my homies. I was dying inside because I felt like nobody cared. I knew that I should not feel this way, but I couldn't figure out how to make it better. So, I kept feeding myself the things of the world to numb the pain of my past. Little did I know I was destroying myself mentally, physically, and emotionally.

When I was thirteen, I had confided in a girlfriend. She was not my first girlfriend, but she was my first long term relationship, and I dated her until I was 18. She was beautiful. I remember the first time we met. A group of my friends were hanging out in the backyard of a friend's house in the shed. The night grew late, everyone began to leave, but she stayed. We stayed up listening to music and talking. She confided in me about the time she was sexually abused, and I confided in her about my sexual abuse. Here we were both barely teenagers, sitting in a shed sharing deep dark secret with each other. I immediately fell in love with her. The night drew on, rain began to fall on the roof of the shed, and we couldn't move away from each other. After that night, she knew everything about me and understood why I would do some of the harmful things I did. Some of the harmful behavior I was engaging in included stabbing the back of my throat, banging my head against brick walls, and jumping in front of a train. I once jumped on the roof of her mother's house while her mother was sleeping and grabbed the power line. I cannot explain why it didn't throw me off the roof or kill me. My reckless behavior was out of control. I didn't realize the source of my pain, but knew I was crying out for help. I needed something in my life to help me. The drugs were not helping, the alcohol was not helping, the sex was not helping, the respect was not helping. I was searching for every inch the world for something to help. I had an emptiness inside that could not be filled by anything of this world.

I didn't fully understand it at the time, but I needed Jesus Christ the true source of redemption. I thought I needed Him to come in and magically fix all my problems. However, now, I know that I needed him to redeem me from all my sin, but I refused to repent and turn away from my sin. It would still be a long time till I was ready to give up my gangster lifestyle and surrender to the Amazing Grace of the Prince of Peace, Jesus Christ.

I was not through my journey yet; I was about to turn eighteen and the charges I had as a juvenile were catching up to me. I never made my court appearances; I was on the run from my probation officer when the police caught me. They arrested me and put me in the back of the cop car. I banged my head against the glass in the car so violently that they sent me to a behavioral health center. While I was there, they put me back on my medications and I started counseling again. I did not like the way the staff treated not only me, but the other patients at the center. They had no compassion; it was like they hated their job. Their treatment of us as patients made me mad. There is a lot of free time in rehab and being in a new environment I would sit back and watch people. I could tell that the employees did not have good characters.

One example of this poor character almost landed me in the padded room. I have a tendency to feel like I need to protect people. I am not sure if it stems from not having a father or life on the streets, but I tend to get in trouble because I feel the urge to defend. One day, all the patience where in a common room and a staff member said something off color to another patient. I got mad and started yelling uncontrollably to the staff member. The staff member reacted by pushing me and he was about to finish up by hitting me when the supervisor stepped in to stop him. I got nervous. Other patience that had run ins with staff members had ended up being sedated and placed in the padded room and I just knew that is where I was headed. Luckily, I never hit the staff member and that is what saved me from the padded room. I was able to go back to my room to cool off.

I did not have very many visitors in rehab. Most of my friends and family didn't understand what I was going through and felt like they couldn't help me. For some reason, my mother contacted the church in our neighborhood. Pastor Ray and Deacon Larry of Victory Baptist Church (VBC) were obedient to God's call to love others, and they made a visit to me in rehab. They told me how Jesus wanted to forgive me of my sins. How Jesus died on the cross to wash all my sins away. I heard this story my entire life, but they presented it to me again and explained it to me with a piece of paper. They wrote some sins on a piece of paper and used it as an example for all the sins I committed against God and against other people. When you repent and ask Jesus to forgive you from these sins, God will forgive you and Jesus' blood will wash away all your sins forever. They flipped the piece of paper over and said my sins were washed away, but first I had to turn away from the way I had been living. I needed to believe that Christ died on the cross and rose from the grave on the third day. I wanted to accept the forgiveness, but I wasn't willing to change my life. I refused the grace of God again. They prayed for me and still loved me even though I didn't accept the free offer of forgiveness through Jesus Christ.

A few days later, my probation officer came to visit with some legal advice. She shared that if I served some time at a rehabilitation facility the judge would probably drop all my charges, but if I didn't go to rehab, I could be tried as an adult, and end up spending close to ten years in prison, so I agreed to go to rehab. They found a place I couldn't run from, and it was four hours away from OKC, way out in the Southeastern part of Oklahoma.

"And this is the condemnation, that the
light has come into the world, and men
loved darkness rather than the light,
because their deeds were evil." John 10:19

CHAPTER 7

NO RESULTS

In the rehabilitation facility, I learned about myself and my addiction. I began to like the sober me. I discovered that I stopped growing emotionally the day I came dependent on alcohol and drugs, I had the emotional age of a 12-year-old at the age of 17. I spent my 18th birthday in the rehab facility. It was one of the most memorable birthdays, I cried whenever the staff surprised me with a birthday cake and sang the birthday song. It wasn't every year I was able to have a cake and a party for my birthday. I know that my mom did the best she could despite her own circumstances, addictions, and trauma, but my 18th birthday party in that facility marked a new beginning for me. I will be forever grateful for my mother's endurance to keep our family together, however, it was time to make some changes.

Three months went by, and I had a new mentality to make drastic changes to my life. I knew that I couldn't be around my old friends if I wanted to stay sober. I knew I had to cut ties when I made it home, but it was more difficult than I expected. Tommy picked me up from my mom's house the day I was release and I immediately relapsed. Tommy tried to be a good influence by telling me I couldn't smoke weed with him, but I insisted. I told him I only went to rehab so I wouldn't have to go to prison, and he laughed. I was now straddling the line between going straight and still living the gangster life from my past. I still desired to have a different life, and I moved in with my girlfriend who I was with since we were 13. I found a construction job that paid $11.00 an hour but it required a clean drug test. I got clean for long enough to pass the drug test. I walked 5 miles to work and back home. I was starting at the bottom, but I thought I was on my way to a good life. I promised my girlfriend we would get our own place and get a car so we wouldn't have to walk anymore. While I was at work, her friends talked her into to being a stripper at the place they worked at, but I was not going to have it. I told her

I loved her but if she started doing that I was going to leave. I couldn't watch her degrade herself. I ended up leaving her because she became a stripper.

I worked at that construction job for about a year and a half. I worked 70 hours a week and was taking home $600 a week after taxes. I bought a car, found a place to rent, but I was still hanging with my homies on my days off. Hanging with my homies meant I was still drinking and doing drugs on the weekends. That is how I lived life until I lost my job, they popped a random drug test on me and of course I failed. I was devastated and I eventually had to move back in with my mother, but I was determined to find another job. My mother suggested I go to my dad's old job to work as a roofer. It was a good suggestion, they put me to work immediately on the hot roofing crew. It provided enough money for me to live in a low-income apartment and I enjoyed having my own place.

One Friday, when the day was almost over, they called for the last few buckets to be filled of hot liquid asphalt. It was my job to fill the buckets and carrying them over to the work spot. I had been doing this all day without incident; however, it was the end of the day, and I was getting tired. Unknowingly, while filling the buckets, my boot melted to the roof, and I stepped back with the buckets and fell. The buckets dropped out of my hands and the five-hundred-degree asphalt splashed onto my face and covered both my eyes. I was running, jumping, and screaming on the corner of the roof. My co-workers kept telling me to be still, that I was going to fall off the roof. It burned so much that I couldn't keep still, and I was scared it was going to burn through my eyelids. Someone quickly suggested to pour iced tea on my face to cool it off. Someone else carried me down the ladder and rushed me to the hospital. The whole time we were on the way to the burn center he was crying and apologizing for what had happened. All he kept saying was that someone should have been helping me. I wasn't scared after the asphalt cooled off, but I still couldn't see because it had melted my eyes shut.

The nurse began to pull the asphalt off my face, and I can't remember if they gave me anything for pain. I just remember talking as if nothing had happened. She pulled enough of it off for me to see her face and I asked her if I was in heaven. She started to blush, and we carried on our conversation. The doctor told me I had to leave my burn exposed for a month.

This would give enough time for the doctor to see how bad I was burned. I waited for the construction supervisor to pick me up and I avoided any car mirrors because I didn't want to see how bad my face was damaged. I am not a vain person, but it was still difficult to face reality. My supervisor was nice during the car ride, he took me to get my medication, brought me my weekly check, and had already filed workman's comp. He made sure I would be taken care of while I recovered.

I was not going to be able to take care of myself during the recovery, so he dropped me off at my mom's house. My sister Tosha was the first one in my family to see me. She walked from the kitchen into the living room to see who walked in the door. She saw my face and started crying. This prompted my mom to walk into the living room and she started crying too. Tosha asked why all the bad stuff always happens to me. I didn't know how bad it was and I didn't really care, all I cared about at that moment was trying to erase the feelings from the long day. At that moment, I believed that the only thing that would make me feel better was taking my pain meds with any form of alcohol. After I finally looked in the mirror, all I could see was the guy off Batman. You know the guy that had half his face burnt off. It was bad, and I was ashamed of the way I looked. I eventually moved back to my apartment where I could be alone, and I started to become depressed. I was taking my medication the psychiatrist gave me, but I was also using drugs and alcohol the whole time. After thirty days, I had an appointment with the burn center, and they scheduled a date for surgery. I evaded the public until I could have surgery. I was scaring people, especially children and I couldn't go to the grocery store or any store for that matter without everyone staring at me. Burning my face intensified the childhood feelings of abandonment and isolation. I pondered on this fact; I was not living life the way God wanted me to live. I was lost and I needed God to seek and save me from myself. (Luke 19:10)

> *"See, I have set before you today life and*
> *good, death and evil, in that I command*
> *you today to love the LORD your God,*
> *to walk in His ways, and to keep His*

commandments, His statutes, and His

judgments, that you may live and

multiply; and the LORD your God will

bless you in the land which you possess."

Deuteronomy 30:15-16

CHAPTER 8

SEARCHING FOR PEACE

Just like when I was trapped in the oven and had been burned by the boiling potatoes, the surgery to repair the burns on my face required a skin graft. The next few months I had a bandage over my entire face, only my right eye and mouth were exposed so I could see, eat, and drink. The medication I was prescribed to help manage the pain caused me to be exhausted most of the time. I learned self-control because I needed to take only the prescribed medicine for pain and not to abuse them. Every week, I had to visit the doctor so they could change my bandages. I was under strict instructions not to take them off myself. My sister, Renea, lived in the same projects, just two buildings away, and she took care of me while I was hurt. One night, I was staying over on her couch, I woke up to use the restroom and while washing my hands the bandages fell off my face. I looked in the mirror and saw thirty staples attaching the skin to my face. I was angry! I didn't know my face looked like Frankenstein's monster stapled together and I began to cry. Devastated, I wondered how I ended up looking like a monster.

I tried to get my life back to normal, but I was not sure what was truly normal. So far, my childhood was anything but normal and here I stood on the verge of being an adult with no direction. All I had was just the pain of tragedy after tragedy. When people came to visit me while I recovered, I would make jokes about my looks instead of being honest about the grief I felt for being disfigured. I knew in my heart that my friends were my true friends, no matter what I looked like, but I still felt alone. I began to fixate on the fact that I probably would never have a girlfriend due to being mutilated. The doctor eventually removed the staples, and I was able to walk around without a bandage. I felt a little normal but was I still insecure. If someone looked at me too long, their stares would make my insecurities flare up again. The doctors said it would take time for the skin graft to blend into the rest of my face and the redness would eventually go away, but it wasn't fast enough for me. The feelings of shame due to the disfigurement continued to consume me. I continued to self-medicate the shame away with drugs and alcohol, now paired with all the different prescriptions for my depression and injury. I eventually ended up going back to work for the same company, but this time they made me the "kettle man" where I put the solid tubes of asphalt into the already liquid asphalt. I was given a full mask to wear over my head and face to protect me. Going back to work did not provide the feeling of normal I was looking for and I chose alcohol and drug use over my job.

I quit my job and lost my apartment mostly because I wanted to stay home and get drunk and high all the time. I moved back to my mother's house, this felt normal. The cycle of stress, alcoholism, and abuse was a dangerous comfort to me. One night my mother, Renea, and I were drinking and playing dominoes. My mother was the first to get drunk and we started to argue. I don't remember what we were arguing about, but she told me I would be a coward just like my dad. I would run from everything and never amount to anything.

I was already in a bad place, so it wasn't hard for me to believe those things about myself. Plus, living with my mom in the cycle of abuse only reminded me of the unresolved issues of my childhood: abandonment, abuse, sodomization, medical trauma. Now my mother was only amplifying the loud voices in my head that told me I was worthless, damaged, and unlovable. I went to the bedroom, grabbed the full prescription (3,000 mg of Trazadone) and took it all. Laying down on the bed, I closed my eyes to the chaos of the world and surrendered to the peace of sleep. I needed peace in my life, and I thought death was the only way I could ever experience it. God had different plans for me, I woke up inside the ambulance to chaos once again. The sharp smack of a hand across my face, slapping me to stay awake. Repeatedly, but I kept surrendering to the peace of sleep.

Finally, I opened my eyes to the walls of a hospital room, to a tube down my throat that was hooked up to a machine helping me breathe. In my hand, I could feel the warmth of someone else. It was my mother sitting next to me holding my hand, her and I made eye contact and she started to cry. Before she left to get the doctor, she told me she loved me and that she was sorry for saying those things to me. Apparently, I had been in a coma for 2 days and was on a breathing machine. The doctor explained a few things to me including that I flatlined a few times. Then he sent everyone out of the room and looked me in the eyes and began to make it clear to me that I shouldn't be alive. He pointed out that God was looking out for me. The machine was breathing for me because all my organs went to sleep, the 3000mg of Trazadone did its job. Before he walked out of the room, he looked right at me and said, "God saved you…"

Two years later, I did it again. Nothing in my life had changed drastically and I was having the same feelings of shame. My mom's boyfriend at the time had been taking the same medication that I had overdosed on before. I asked him if I could borrow some to help me sleep. I had been on cocaine and meth and hadn't been able to sleep. My mom was asleep in her room, and he brought the whole bottle to me. I took it from him and took all that he had. He witnessed my taking all the pills and ran to go wake up my mom. Oblivious to the world around me, I made a phone call to my friend Lissa. In an emotional and drug induced state, I began to apologize to her for overdosing. Unknowingly to me, Lisa had hung up on me to call 911. once again, I shut my eyes to the chaos of the world in search of peace.

This time, I woke up to nine of my homies gathered around my bed saying their goodbyes because I had been in a coma for three days. They started crying and told me if I ever needed to talk, I should call them. I didn't think they would ever understand all the secrets I was holding inside. I was at a different hospital and had a different doctor who ran everyone out of the room. When the doctor and I were alone, he began to ask me questions and I could only nod "yes or no" because I was hooked up to a breathing machine with a tube down my throat again. At the end of the questioning, the doctor looked me in the eye and said, "God has a plan for you because you shouldn't be alive, and I heard this is not the first time."

"The Lord is not slack concerning His
promise, as some would count slackness,
but is longsuffering toward us, not willing
that any should perish but that all should
come to repentance." 2 Peter 3:9

CHAPTER 9

DIGGING A HOLE

Two attempted suicides should have been a wakeup call, but I continued to dig a hole for myself that would be nearly impossible to escape without the divine intervention of God. The gangster lifestyle was ingrained in me since I was a child and to me being a gangster was the measure of success. When I was in middle school, I remember visiting two of my uncles in prison. Both were in the same prison for different reasons and doing a long stretch of time. They were both artists and they put their money together to purchase paints. Together they painted a mural inside the prison on the rec wall. It depicted a beautiful skyscape that inspired me. I had only ever witnessed failures in my family. This mural was the first time I can remember anyone in my family being successful at something and the bond that my uncles, from different sides of my family, shared over the mural was also something I had never witnessed before. It made me believe that life was better in prison. That someone like me could only be successful in prison. At that moment, I wanted to be just like them, I wanted to go to prison. After all, the rappers glorified it and made it sound cool. It was the closest thing I had to a dream or a life goal, but I eventually found out the truth about prison. I never had anyone I looked up to and never had a dad in my life to show me right from wrong. All of my years, I never had someone to encourage me when I made good grades or tell me that if I kept my life straight that I could go somewhere or become someone. Instead, the opposite was influencing me and the gangster state of mind consumed my every thought.

Time seemed to fly by as the drugs took over my life and addiction returned. It wasn't that I couldn't function without drugs, but the fact that I couldn't get away from them. I was stuck in a hole and couldn't leave it even if I wanted. I was trapped in a cycle, deceived by the temptation of women, drugs, alcohol, guns, respect, gang affiliation, and status. I glorified gangster life and the consequences seemed just as much fun. I was blinded by the power and control I thought I had over my life.

I do not want to glorify any of the things that I did while I was a part of a gang, but I want to share my mind frame at the time so people can better understand how far I have come. I would not encourage any of the lifestyle that I lived. Families were hurt during the course of my gangster journey. I never considered the fact that my selfishness would influence my own family. My siblings eventually followed in my footsteps, and I regret every moment they were influenced by me. Another regret is that I did not take a stand against this generational curse sooner. It needed to stop with me, a new influence could have been started, but I ignored the call to make a difference in society. We are society! In order for a change to happen, I had to change, and you must change as well. Unfortunately, I did not change at this point in my life, instead I continued to dig that hole.

Let me share just how deep of a hole I dug by sharing some of my charges. Again, I am not glorifying any of it;

I want you to understand the power of God in rescuing a sinner like me. He delivered me from every bad choice I made in my life, choices that I thought could never be forgiven or redeemed.

In 2003, I lived with my girlfriend Lissa who was also living with the mother of my best friend Tommy's children. The kids were busting beer bottles in the street, so the police came for a welfare check. They found a sawed-off shotgun and another gun way up in the top cabinet. Even though it was out of reach of the children; they threatened to take the kids away if someone didn't claim the illegal sawed-off shotgun. I admitted that all the guns were mine including the sawed-off shotgun and I was charged with my first felony. I was charged with Possession of Sawed-Off Shotgun. I jumped bond a few times by not showing up for court and eventually did six months on this charge.

Then in 2004, I was living with a different girl, Marie, we met after I got out of county jail. She and I started to have a disagreement because she had spent several days with another man. We broke up because of this conflict and I moved out into Tommy's house which we called The

Spot. The Spot was a single family- blue house that was central to everything we did in the gang. A few days after I moved in with Tommy, she found me and began threatening to burn all my belongings I had left behind at her house. She kept coming back time and time again begging me to get back with her, I dodged her threats until one night, when she snuck into The Spot and followed me out the back door. She kept harassing me despite the fact I was telling her to leave me alone. I walked down the street and began to jump fences to escape to the next block. She drove around the block and found me there. It was three in the morning, and not wanting to draw attention to us, I got into the car. I had not seen her for a few days, and I didn't know what was in the car with her. As we pulled away; and got a few blocks down the road the police shined their spotlight into the car. Immediately, I could see the glow of the red and blue lights flashing behind me. The police pulled us over because I wasn't wearing my seatbelt. Panic began to rise from the backseat as one of Marie's friends freaked out. Her hands were shaking as she tried to pass a bunch Xanax bars up to Marie in the front seat. Xanax bars are the street name for the most potent Xanax on the medical market. Nervous and scared, she spilled them all over the front seat. Suspicious of our behavior and the large number of pills spilt in the front seat, the police yanked me out the car first to search me. Luckily, I didn't have anything on me, but they found some digital scales under my seat and assumed they were mine. They started to ask me about a murder related to all the gang shootings that had recently happened. Next, they called a lady officer to search Marie; they found a large bag of meth with little bags of meth inside. Even though I didn't have any drugs on me, I was charged with Possession of Controlled Substance with Intent to Distribute (CDS w/ Intent). I had only gotten into the car five minutes before trying to get away from Marie. While during my life I was certainly guilty of distributing drugs, in this moment I was not. At the time, I felt like I was wrongly charged, but this is what happens when you live a life surrounded by drugs and illegal activity. Mere proximity can land you in jail, plus I had a reputation and a rap sheet that the cops could not deny my involvement with drugs. I bonded out, I went back to The Spot. Gang life started to grow more and more dangerous as shootings began to happen more regularly at The Spot. For example, rival gangs would shoot at people while they were picking up drugs. One time, a child was peppered with a buckshot outside of the house, and another time a homie was shot 6 times. The Spot was riddled with bullet holes in the sides of the house many of them only two inches apart. Rival gangs regularly drove by the Spot to threaten our gang by shooting before they made it to the front of the house. This made the neighborhood one of the most dangerous in the city. There was a week of two-a-day drive-by shootings and one of those days I had to jump onto a child to protect them from getting hit by stray bullets. I would sit on the porch waiting and watching, and I would be shot at multiple times a day. Two of my other homies were shot at their house in a drug robbery. Violence was all around me. I was getting jumped, not only outside of jail, but inside of jail. There was nowhere to run to get away from the violence that engulfed my life. I was wanted by the police and wanted by rival gangs. I was always watching and living by instinct. Every decision I made could have meant life or death for me and others. Unknown cars, cars driving fast, I knew they were coming to shoot up the place and I would pull my strap ready to bust back. Every moment of my life was intense, and I was living very guarded. I think the only thing keeping me from being institutionalized due to the pressure of the violence around me was that I had a small hope for something better. I am grateful I knew there was hope for something better in life, but there was only one problem, I still wasn't ready to repent.

"But God demonstrates His own love towards us, in that while we were still sinners Christ died for us." Romans 5:8

CHAPTER 10

DIGGING A DEEPER HOLE

Caught up in the identity of being a gangster I felt I had no other options then to continue the journey I was already traveling. Instead of repenting from all my sins and turning away from that lifestyle, I made a daily choice to hang out with my gang in all the wrong places. One night the police walked in the door of The Spot while we were partying, and we were caught off guard. The Gang Task Force always harassed us because of our previous encounters with the police. This time, I had all the drugs on me, and I had stashed a pistol under the cushion of the couch where I was sitting. The task force aggressively asked everyone to stand up and slowly walk outside, except for me. The taskforce sergeant told me to stay in my seat and he mocked me saying, "Don't worry about this guy, he is digging a hole for himself, literally." The same sergeant had responded to the calls of my other arrests, and he figured I was no factor in the gang. Little did he know that I was the only one with the drugs, money, and gun that night. No one went to jail that evening and I thank God I was never searched. Even though I continued to place myself in dangerous and illegal situations God still protected me.

I was running from bounty hunters because I jumped bond on the CDS w/Intent, but life on the run didn't mean anything to me. I was always running from something. One day, Tommy and I were hanging out as usual at The Spot. It was about noon when Tommy and I had just finished smoking a joint together. After we smoked, he got in the shower, and I laid down on the bed. I watched as the sun filled the bedroom from all the windows and the effects of the marijuana consumed my mind. Soon, I began to hear the jingle of keys and footsteps outside the window. Not sure if the drugs were playing trick in my mind or if there was really someone outside, I began to sit up out of bed to look out the window. Just as I registered what I was seeing, Tommy walked out of the bathroom and saw the same thing I did, cops surrounding the place. I remember looking into Tommy's eyes and feeling like we could hear each other's thoughts. In that peaceful moment, we both knew that we would not see each other for a very long time. The peace quickly faded into chaos as the cops began yell at us to put our hands up. Quickly they cuffed and separated us as they searched the house; then they began to question us about the drugs and gang. These cops were a part of the Alcohol Tobacco Firearms (ATF) and Gang Task Force (GFT) and they knew everything about our gang. They had been investigating us for a long time. Some of the officers were the same ones that responded to my suicide attempts. Because they knew so much about us, they began to mock us. They knew how far gone we were, and they treated us as such by spitting on us and calling us names. Once the questioning was over, they put us both in the back of the same cop car. The cops inside the car began to talk trash on my suicide attempts and I could feel the anxiety began to rise inside me as I looked for something to bang my head on. In a quiet moment during the ride to the jail, Tommy yelled, "I smell bacon! Take off that uniform and I bet you are still a punk!" The patrol car pulled into the Oklahoma County Jail where they put both of us in a holding cell. Tommy made a phone call for some help, but I had no one to call. I remember one of the guards coming around the corner to our cell holding red jumpsuits. Red jumpsuits indicate that you have a federal case against you. I knew enough to know that there was no way I had federal case against me, but I complied anyway. Soon they moved me to the 12th floor to await trail. The 12th floor was solitary confinement and it housed murders and rapists. I have been in the presence of a lot of different evil in my life, but I could feel the evil on that floor, and it was a feeling that still sticks with me. I waited 3 months for a trial. I ended up being sentenced to 1 year in county jail and 9 years suspended sentence. I ended up serving 15 months because I didn't get credit for the 3 months I served as I waited for the trial. Tommy didn't fare so well. He got sentenced to 10 years of federal prison. Tommy already had priors and he was on his last chance. The thought of his four kids not seeing him for a long time and how he would never get those years of his kid's life back tore me up. I cried in my cell thinking about how I helped raise his kids and I knew the struggle of their mother's addiction to cocaine. Bearing the responsibility of my actions was something I struggled with, that is how I knew there had to be a better way to live. As far back as I could remember, I always felt responsible whenever a homeboy was killed or put into prison. I had a conscience and knew I was part of the problem because I participated in the gang. I was responsible, I was part of the cause, and now I see the effects it has on families, but still, I did not repent and turn to Jesus despite the internal struggle I was having.

My last charge was After Former Conviction of Firearm (AFC) in 2006. A homeboy was killed, and the family had suspicions it was his girlfriend who set him up to be murdered by a rival gang. He was shot at a convenience store at 6 a.m. on his way to work. His girlfriend knew his routine, he always stopped at the same store every morning to get breakfast. A lot of us speculated that she was a buster and had tipped off the rival gang. However, there was no physical evidence to link her to the murder. A few months passed, and she started hanging out with my gang.

One night she asks for a ride so me and another guy plus one of her friends jump in a car to give her a ride. I was suspicious of her and very guarded when she was around. We dropped her off at a house and her friend wanted to stay the night with me. The next day the friend that stayed with me wanted to go check on the friend we had dropped off at a house the night before. It did not sit well with me, and I was suspicious that I was being set up. I didn't know anything about the house where we had been the previous night and I was always paranoid of rival gangs and bounty hunters. We pull up to the house and she starts to get out of the car. She pauses right as she is about to lift out of the seat and looks back and me. I could see the fear in her eyes and my need to protect her began to far outweigh my need to protect myself. At first, she wanted me to go up and knock on the door of the house, but I was not an idiot. I compromised with her and walked to the sidewalk just outside the house. A 13 yr. old came out on the porch and told us her friend was in the backyard. The friend begged me to walk with her to the backyard and before I passed the front corner of the house, I looked back at the porch and ten gang members walked out of the house. I knew I should have not left the car, but it was too late.

The rival gang members were now between me and the car I was riding in, and I knew right then I had been set up. I started to walk back to the car around the group, but they were questioning who I was because all gangs are territorial. To intimidate me, they started throwing beer bottles at me until I answered them. I finally stopped and tried to explain that I didn't mean any disrespect. They kept trying to hit me with bottles, so I gave in, and I told them my name and what hood I was from. Overlapping the chaos of the beer bottles, the two girls started to throw punches against each other defending their rival gangs. Apparently, neither of the girls realized they were connected to rival gangs. I tried to grab the one girl that was with me and get her back into the car, but shots rang out. I could hear the bullets hitting the car as I ran through the crossfire and jumped into the passenger seat. I didn't know the driver and he had his head tucked under the steering wheel screaming in fear. I was trying to put the car into reverse, but he didn't have his foot on the brake, and I kept yelling "put your foot on the brake!". One of the girls had her nose shot off and a guy was shot in the leg. The girl almost died because she couldn't breathe, and we almost went down for murder. Two days later, the Gang Task Force ran in my mother's house looking for me with shotguns to her head as they had her on the ground. She told them where she thought I was and they found me. I was booked on two Shooting w/ intent, Kidnapping, and AFC of a Firearm.

The District Attorney (D.A.) dropped the charges for Shooting with Intent and Kidnapping because with some integrity, the girl testified in court that I was only trying to protect her from being shot. They found the shooter, but it still left me with the AFC which carried a mandatory ten years. I was still on probation for the last two charges. I had a five-year suspended sentence running concurrent with a ten-year suspended sentence after serving time on both previous charges. I was in a world of trouble, and I knew I was in going to prison for a long time. No gun was found on me, but two witnesses testified seeing me at the scene of the shooting. The D.A. had a solid case because "I knowingly and willing" got into the car and was not supposed to be in "1,500 feet of a firearm". I don't know what else I was supposed to do because the only safe place at the time was in the car and I didn't know there was a gun in the car.

Trapped in a cell in the Oklahoma County Jail, I patiently waited for my court hearings that happened about every month. No bondsman would touch my bond because I jumped bond on the other charges more than a few times and I had a track record of running. On the first court date they offered me twenty years in prison, the next month they offered me seventeen years in prison and three years out on probation, and the last offer was fifteen years in and five years out. My future was setting like the sun behind a chain-link fence of the jail. The gang status I had dreamed of since I visited my uncles in jail was finally coming true and I knew that I was going to die in prison.

"For all have sinned and fall short of the
glory of God" Romans 3:23

CHAPTER 11

A GLIMPSE OF HOPE

I was very good at making enemies and I did not care who I offended while I was locked up. I was either going to kill someone in a jail gang fight or someone was going to kill me. It was no different than being on the streets and with this much time to serve, I wasn't going to make it out of prison. I started to have the mindset of defeat, but I coped the best way I could with humor. All the inmates in my pod would come hang out in my cell to share funny stories at night to pass the time. I would tell stories like this one....

One dark night, I pulled up to Tommy's apartment and a guy thought I broke into his car and pulled a shotgun on me. I walked him backwards to his apartment and I was telling him to shoot me. I heard the brakes squeak from the police cars, and I ran. I don't know why I ran because I didn't do anything illegal, but I knew I had a complicated relationship with cops. I ran to hide in the bushes, and I quickly texted Tommy to pick me up after the police left. He responded to my text and told me to jump in the car when he pulled up. Headlights were coming and I ran for my life praying I would make it to Tommy's car before the cops or the angry neighbor saw me. Baggy jeans are cool and all but try to run in them and you will soon realize why athletes don't wear them. My feet got tangled up in my pants, and I fell right before I could see what kind of car it was. Out of breath, eyes watering, I got in and sitting next to me was a cop. Everyone in the cell erupted with laughter. All my life, I was trying desperately to be the cool smooth gangster, and as I sat in jail thinking, I recognized for the first time that I was just everyone's clown.

I had hours to think about all the times someone had played me the fool. I had been set up, charged for things I didn't do, and I felt that the women in my life used me for drugs. The life that I had lived up to this point was a joke. To commemorate my revelation, I got tattoos on my face of "Tears of a Clown." I was hiding my pain behind the exterior of my meaningless laughter and smiles. I put them on my face because I thought I was never going to be out in society ever again. I was mentally preparing to spend a long time, if not the rest of my life in prison. I knew I had made choices that had ultimately brought me to prison, and I was beginning to regret the choices I made to ignore my family, friends, pastors, and deacons that tried to speak truth into my life. I knew my choice to ignore them left me with no hope.

There was a familiar face in jail, a guy who would buy marijuana from us was on his way out of jail. As he was being escorted out of the pod, he looked back at me and said, "I will do everything I can to make your bond happen." I yelled back, "Don't make empty promises." A few days later I had a visitor who I refused to see because it was not visitation day. The only time you get visitors on non-visitation days is if you are being interrogated by detectives. I refused the visitor, but the guard said he would drag me if I didn't come with him. Everything I got away with rushed through my mind as I was taken to the 1st floor where the mirrored interrogation room waited. I just knew I was going to be questioned for one of the other many crimes I had committed. The guard walked me past those rooms, I started to be confused as he put me in a regular visitation room. There was a short old lady on the other side of the glass, and I picked up the phone as she asked if I was Emmitt. I confirmed and the next question flabbergasted me because she asked if I wanted to bond out of jail!

Before she proceeded, she asked me to look into her eyes and promise her I would show up for court and explained to me that if I missed one court date that her house would be in the bondsman's possession. My friend had really come through on his promise to bond me out of jail and he even got his mother to her house up as collateral for my bond. Caught off-guard by her offer, I sat there thinking about it for a while. I was a decent enough human being to understand that if I was going to run, it was best if didn't take her offer to bond out. I was going to keep my promise because I thought if I could get out of jail, I would have a better chance to fight my case with a lawyer rather than a court ordered public defender.

Once I was out of jail, the lawyers I contacted wanted me to make a plea deal with the D.A. to serve some time, but I wanted to take it to trial so I wouldn't have to do any time. I knew I wasn't guilty of all the charges filed against me. However, no one wanted to fight because the D.A. had a solid case against me. If the case, went to trail I could lose and be made an example of by a judge. I had heard of a guy from our neighborhood that took his case to trial, lost it, and the judge gave him 120 years in prison to scare other ganger members. His family was devastated, and I knew it was a big possibility it could happen to me. At the time of the shoot-out, I didn't know that getting into the car with a firearm or being within fifteen hundred feet of a firearm would violate my probation. I was determined to fight the case and found a lawyer named Elton. I made a down payment, and we began to meet regularly to talk about the case.

Elton advised me to keep my nose clean meaning to stay out of trouble. My defense for the case was to try and prove to the court's that I could be a functioning citizen in society. I was required to meet my probation officer every week for drug tests. I was put into a program where I had to be in a meeting every week with others like myself with a court related counselor for a year. I was court ordered to a 10 week "Life Skills" class which included a victim's impact panel session. The judge saw all the progress I was making and had compassion for me. I still remember Judge Black's face as he spoke with me and gave me a second chance. Instead of jail time, the court ordered me to a construction trade school for a year. I enrolled into G.E.D. classes and I was determined to prove myself. I was satisfied with not being in jail to say the least, but it still didn't make things right with God. The grace that Judge Black showed me changed my life. The same can be true for you, reader, God is giving you the gift of grace if you repent and turn from the sin in your life.

> *"As it is written: There is none righteous,*
> *no, not one; There is none who*
> *understands; There is none who seeks after*
> *God, they have all turned aside."*
> *Romans 3:10-11*

CHAPTER 12

DEMONS AND ADDICTION

(BATTLE OVER DARKNESS)

Early in the book, I described my life as a violent storm. I think at this point you see the evidence of a dark violent storm over my life. The darkness of a family legacy of alcohol abuse, the darkness of gang life, the darkness of drug abuse, the darkness that drove me to suicide, but the darkest part of my life had yet to come. I was about to embark on a battle to improve my life on my own to try to overcome the darkness on my own. As I tried to take steps forward to turn my life around the darkness would return with vengeance and push me all the way back to the starting line. The repetitiveness of failing drove me deeper into drugs which started to affect my mind and spirit.

My whole life depended on what the judge decided, and once everything was said and done, I had fought the case for three years. I still had a drug addiction and alcohol problem. The lifestyle still existed even though I knew my future was on the line. I had got into a car wreck drinking and driving, pulled over while being high on meth, and ticketed twice for driving under suspension. I passed every drug test but only because I knew exactly how long the drugs stayed in my system and would schedule my drug intake around my drug tests. I completed everything the judge asked of me, and the D.A. lowered the charge to Carrying Weapons and was given 30 days in jail. I caught a lucky break because I had some construction work from my previous jail sentence, and I ended up only served 12 days of the 30. The judge put me on another 10-year suspended sentence not before he looked at me said he better not see me in court ever again.

It was 2009 and following all the legal trouble I had a strong desire to get my life right. I had a girlfriend named Vero who I was off and on with since 2004. We loved each other. She had been with me through part of my convictions and supported me during my jail time. Once I got out of jail, we lived together. I remember feeling the urge to get sober and escape the lifestyle I had been living. However, Vero did not share the vision I did. So, we would argue all the time. We were not good influences on each other. I was struggling with sobriety and was not pleasant to be around. She was still using drugs regularly and didn't understand why I wanted to get sober. I wish I could tell you that I was successful at being sober, but he darkness over my life drew me back to drugs time and time again. Vero and I started to use drugs more regularly together. We would go on multiple day benders between drug tests. We would get high on meth and cocaine and not sleep for 2 or 3 days. These benders started to affect my mind and I started to become even more paranoid. At first, I couldn't explain what was happening. I thought Vero was sneaking around with another man. I would run around the house with a knife and a gun thinking she was hiding someone. I had been cheated on by most of the females in the past and the females I was fooling around with were cheating on their boyfriends or husbands. I knew how deceitful a women could be, and

I knew how deceitful I was, but soon I realized there was something darker about my paranoia.

I was beginning to witness the spiritual battle for my soul as I was inching toward the seed of the gospel taking root; Satan was pulling me back into the darkness of sin. The first time I encountered demons was when Vero and I first started dating and I stayed up all night high on drugs. I began to see demons walking around as I laid next to Vero, and I watched as a huge demon ducked its head and turn sideways just to fit into the door. Two others followed it in the room, and I sat up and pulled out my knife. The little one jumped on the bed and the other one approached the bed, and I started swinging the knife trying to cut it. All of the movement caused Vero to wake up, she started scream-ing and crying at the sight of me trying to stab nothing. She turned on the light and the demons disappeared. She was visibly upset, and it made me think that she was upset because she saw the demons too. So, I asked her. All she could do was cry, pull me close to her and beg me to lay back down and go to sleep. She didn't understand what was happening and maybe she just thought I was having a bad trip. She turned the lights back off and there were the demons standing in the exact same places as before. I jumped up trying to swing at them. Eventually, we left the lights on so I could go to sleep.

I had another encounter with a demon, and I started to believe that I was possessed. I was trying to sleep-off a three-day bender on meth when I felt an immense pressure on my back. I jumped up and ran out the apartment and didn't go back until later that evening. I stopped at a liquor store, went back to the apartment thinking I was going to punk this demon out and fight it. I had a plan to fight this demon. First, I went over to the radio to turn on hard rap, then I began to drink all the liquored I had bought. Feeling in the zone, I started to scream at the demon. Hurling insults into the air trying to taunt the demon so I could fight it face-to-face. Eventually I had too much to drink and blacked out. When I came to my senses, I was holding onto a nurse's shirt begging her not to leave me alone. I have no memory of what happened or why I was picked up by the police. I was terrified as the doctors and the police officer assessed the situation. Soon, they hoisted me on to a hospital bed, tied me down and the nurse pressed a needle into my skin. That was my last memory, the next day the police took me to a crisis center.

One of the last encounters I had was when Vero and I were moving out of our house. Since we were off and on all the time, I had suspicion she had been sneaking someone in the house while we were gone. Things would be moved around the house causing me to be more observant and paranoid. We were in the process of putting things into a storage unit when I had a bright idea to leave an old cell phone in the house to record everything while we were gone. I made this plan without her knowing because I wanted to catch her red-handed cheating on me. I was finally going to have my proof and prove that I was not crazy. While she was carrying a load to the car, I snuck over to the fireplace. One either side of the fireplace hung light fixtured with cloudy glass covers and I placed the recording cell phone inside the light cover. We left to take the load to the storage unit, we quickly unloaded everything, and headed back to the house. The entire drive back, I was trying to think of a way to listen to the recording without her knowing. As we pulled into the driveway, she looks over at me and conveniently states her intent to take a shower. It was a perfect opportunity to hear what I had recorded, and I was eager to listen to it because I was going to catch her sneaking people in and out the house.

I started to play back the recording. I could hear us leaving the house: the lock of the door, the screen door slamming, and the car starting and leaving the driveway. I listened for about three minutes then I heard a loud boom that rattled the clouded glass around the phone. It sounded like an explosion and then I heard steps like a horse or a goat, it walked straight to the fireplace and was breathing hard. I shivered and thought this couldn't be real and then it started to walk off into the kitchen and there was another loud explosion. I had the same eerie feeling that made the hair on my skin stand up just like the other time I had encounters with demons. We hadn't smoked any meth that day and I didn't say anything to Vero because she already thought I was crazy. I got the courage up to ask her mother to listen to it and she refused. Finally, I asked Vero to listen to it, but she also refused. I had my evidence that I wasn't crazy, but nobody would listen to the recording. I was so freaked out by the recording that I destroyed the phone because I didn't want the demon following me around. I know there is a heaven and a hell because I encountered the unseen spiritual world and I have felt the battle for my soul.

"For we do not wrestle against flesh and
blood, but against principalities, against
powers, against rulers of the darkness
of this age, against spiritual hosts of
wickedness in the heavenly places."
Ephesians 6:12

CHAPTER 13

WITH OR WITHOUT YOU

As the battle for my soul raged, another battle emerged within my relationship with Vero. We continued to get high on the weekends and hang out with old friends. Deep down inside I wanted to stop because I was sick of the roller coaster of breaking up, always watching my back, being paranoid of going back to jail, hearing and seeing demons, and being told I was crazy. I knew what sober was, but I was battling with alcoholism and addiction and so was Vero. I promised to marry her and help get custody of her kids but we both had problems we couldn't overcome. We would do well until the weight of all our problems pushed us back into the comfort of drugs and we were back to square one. I hated what the drugs would do to our relationship because I know we loved each other but we continued to hurt each other. After seven years, she gave me an ultimatum, it was either marry her or she was going to end the relationship forever.

Once she gave me the ultimatum, I thought that a commitment to each other would help us stay together despite the cycle of addiction we were living in. We started to plan a wedding. We wanted to get married around the time we began dating which we both remembered to be sometime before Halloween. We decided on October 14th and time was inching closer. We had sent out invitations, her family purchased the cake, I found a venue, I had a tuxedo, and she had her dress. This white wedding, we were planning had a darkness over it, for me, our drug use made our upcoming vows to each other meaningless. How could we love each other unconditionally if both of us loved drugs more? While these doubts circled my mind, I was blinded with excitement. I was excited at the possibility of having a family. I was going to have a wife who came with kids. I never thought I was ever going to have a family of my own. Between my scared face and a birth defect I couldn't believe the day was coming when I would have both. However, I was disappointed by the fact I would never have kids of my own because of the birth defect.

A few days after I was born, I was rushed to the hospital and had double hernia surgery. The doctor told my parents that I would never be able to have children. A fact my parents never revealed to me. Finally, my parents were forced to tell me the truth because I couldn't figure out why I had been with multitudes of women, but they never seemed to get pregnant. I asked my mother, and she finally told me the truth. I had mixed emotions because my homies were getting hit with child support and I had even paid child support for a kid that was not mine. But the fact remained that the heaviness of not being able to have children of my own weighed on my heart and mind. Vero had 2 children who I loved deeply. They would visit on the weekends because she no longer had custody of them. I love kids and I hated that I couldn't have any of my own. At least I could be around and help her with the kids. I have always carried a burden to help women. It stems from watching my mom struggle as a single parent. I am a protector and a fierce warrior. Not just a warrior looking for a fight, but a warrior who fights to protect. I felt strongly that I needed to protect Vero and I think that is why I thought I loved her so deeply. However, I wasn't in a place to protect anyone, and our relationship continued to grow toxic.

As time drew close to the wedding date, I gave her an ultimatum. I told her if I was going to marry her then we needed to move out of OKC to start a new life and get away from the drug culture. I knew that we needed to escape the cycle of addiction and I thought the best way was to run away from all the bad influences in our lives. Vero was not excited about the plan to move. She was worried she would miss visitation with her kid, and I promised her I would bring her back twice a month for visitation. I told her that I was leaving with or without her because I was tired of living trapped in the cycle of addiction, manipulation, paranoia, and abuse. A week before the wedding, I backed out. All the reason I had for wanting to start a new life began to outweigh the love I had for Vero. God began to open my eyes just a little bit, and I came to realize that I would never fully escape the cycle of addiction and abuse if I married someone caught in the same cycle.

For two weeks I heard nothing from Vero, until she broke the silence with a text. She unloaded every hurtful feeling into a constant flow of text messages. Each text more hurtful than the one before. I knew she was trying to hurt me just as bad as I had hurt her by callingof the wedding. The fact is that I never intended to hurt her, she was just part of an old life that I needed to leave behind. She texted me that I made her look ridiculous, that she hated me, and would never forgive me. She went on and on about how she wished I would die then maybe she would feel better. She kept saying I was schizophrenic and that she was crazy herself for ever falling in love with me. At the time I was seeking to better myself, but I was still drinking. I had been going to narcotics anonymous meetings, but it was not helping. I began to drink a lot in those two weeks. Drinking and drugs where the only way I knew how to deal with strong emotions. I was lost, but somehow felt like I was making the right choices by trying to leave that life behind. My family was my biggest support during that time. They encouraged me to stay away from Vero, to let her heal from the embarrassment of calling off the wedding. I felt like a failure, and I began to think about having a shoot-out with the police, that is when I knew I needed help. I needed someone to help me because my life had been nothing but a string of cruel jokes.

I needed a safe place to figure out my life and the only place that I could think of was rehab. I went to my mother's house and asked her to help find me a rehab that would take me quickly. She called around to a few different rehabs and the next day found a place that had an opening. I remember that I could check in on the day before Halloween. The problem was I needed to find a way to Tulsa. Vero called me for some reason, so I told her I was going to rehab. Surprisingly, she was supportive and offered to give me a ride to the bus station. Now, I just had to find the money to purchase a bus ticket. The only option I had was to call my dad, who I didn't have the best relationship with at that point in my life. He had the nerve to ask me if I was ever going to get right and it hurt because he thought he had the right to speak into my life. The life I had because I had to grow up without the guidance, discipline, and encouragement that a father would have normally provided. In the end, he paid for my bus ticket.

"For I know the thoughts that I think towards you, says the LORD, thoughts of peace and not of evil, to give you a future and a hope." Jeremiah 29

CHAPTER 14

THE BEST DAY OF MY LIFE

As I got ready to leave for rehab, I remember feeling overcome with the sense of embarrassment. I couldn't believe I had let my addiction take over my life. I started to wonder about what my friends and family would think about me. No one in my family ever acknowledged the disease of addiction and I was worried that they would think I wasn't the same Emmitt after I got back from rehab. Part of me knew that I was saying goodbye to my life, my friends, and my family. When I got back from rehab, I knew I would have to limit my time around them if I was ever going to be successful at sobriety. I packed four pairs of clothes in a bag and that was everything I had to my name. Everything that Vero and I had built during our relationship, I left to her. As I placed each item in a bag, I began to realize how selfish it was to think about suicide. I was so concerned about my feelings and how I could make it all go away that I never thought about the effects my death would have on those around me. I began to cry, and my tears confirmed that rehab was the best thing for me at the time. I needed help and I was seeking to get right but in reality; I didn't know where to start. In the N.A. meetings, I kept hearing addiction was a disease, but to me it was like I was stuck in the past. I couldn't keep my head in the past because the past trauma in my life was killing me. I wanted to be free and never call myself a recovering addict or alcoholic because I wanted to be delivered from it all. I was seeking help and little did I know I would find it.

The morning I left for rehab; Vero pulls up to my mom's house. I was struggling to take the first steps of even getting in the car. After some encouragement, we get in the car and drive 7 miles to the bus station in downtown OKC. I went in to purchase my ticket and when I came out, she handed my clothes to me, hugged me, and she barley looked at me as she said, "I have to hurry and leave." Hurry and leave to do what? It was right then and there I knew her love for me faded. I thought our final moments together would be like the movies. In my head, she would sit on the bench crying and waving as the bus pulled away. I envisioned me hanging out of the bus window trying to hold on to the very last image I would ever see of her. It did not go down like that. It hurt because I left everything to her and I thought we still might mean something to each other. Up to that moment, I still had hope for our love. Maybe I thought she would wait for me to get sober, and we would overcome all the odds and still end up together. Instead, I saw the cold hard truth and I was devastated.

As I waited for the bus my mind was overcome with emotions. I thought about Vero and the life I was leaving behind. It was overwhelming as a battle raged inside of me and I had to force myself to sit when all I wanted to do was run. Out of the corner of my eye I could see a gentleman staring at me. He had two different colored eyes and dressed like he was always traveling. I tried my best not to say anything to him because I didn't want to be rude, but I wanted to ask if he knew me or something. He just kept staring at me as if he knew everything about me.

The bus eventually came, and we loaded up to begin the ride to Tulsa, Oklahoma. The battle in my mind continue to rage, I was having mixed emotions wondering why my ex-fiancé was in a hurry to drop me off. I figured she was already seeing someone else, but I loved her, and I still had hope that once I finished rehab, we could work things out. My emotions and thoughts got the best of me and the bus wasn't but twenty miles into the trip when I grabbed my bag and started down the aisle. The unknown traveler, who was staring at me earlier, was in the seat in front of me. I began to yell at the bus driver to let me out as the unknown traveler cut me off mid-sentenced to ask me if I wanted to watch a movie. I was on the verge of a major life decision; sitting down to watch a movie meant a new life, getting off that bus meant returning to the same unhealthy relation-ship.

I didn't want to be rude, so I sat next to him, and he gave me an earbud and we watched a movie. The movie was the comedy 10,000 BC which was not exactly the life changing movie one might assume it would have been. But it changed my life. It took my mind off things until the bus pulled into Tulsa. There was no way for me to get back to OKC now, I had no money. I thanked the unknown traveler for asking me to watch the movie. I quickly shared with him that I was about to get off the bus and he said, "I know". We both stood up and exited the bus. I don't know his name, where he was going, but he changed my life forever. Right outside the bus door there was a taxi waiting to take me directly to rehab for two weeks. When I arrived at rehab, I began now familiar routine of checking into rehab. This was not my first visit to rehab, but it would be my last. The stripped me of my cell phone, belt, shoestrings, and other items I could have used to hurt myself. The took all my clothes to wash them. Sitting in a hospital gown, they drew blood, evaluated me, and set up my meds.

I was placed in a room with a roommate and given a schedule. There were three mandatory classes in the morning, three in the afternoon, and chapel was voluntary. Chapel was at 8 a.m. and at 6 p.m. I started attending the chapel services every morning and every night. One of the first nights in my rehab stay, I rededicated my life to Christ. I thought I was saved because I said a prayer when

I was a child. I thought I was saved because I was baptized. I thought I was a Christian. The problem was I was never really saved to begin with because I never truly repented of my sins and change the way I lived. So how could a rededicate my life to something I never dedicated my life to. My counselor told me I needed more than two weeks of rehab to fix nineteen years of drug and alcohol abuse. Against the advice of my counselor, I made plans in my head to go back to OKC as soon as possible. After all I was still on probation for another eight years and that meant, I would have to check in with my probation officer.

One night, about a week into my rehab stay, my roommate made fun of me in front of everyone and they all laughed. I told him to meet me in the room because no one disrespects me. I took off towards our room and planned to take my frustration and embarrassment out on the guy that made fun of me. As I raced towards our room all the anger I kept bottled up and suppressed by drugs and alcohol came boiling to the surface. I never asked to be born and especially into the problems I grew up with. All the painful memories flooded my mind: my dad leaving, my mom saying hurtful things to me when she was drunk, the sexual and physical abuse I endured. I was furious and I ran through the door of the room and ran straight to one wall. As I approached the wall, I pulled my arm back, balled my hand into a fist, and punched the wall with all my force. I jerked my hand backed to my side, turned around, lowered my head, and took off full speed to the other wall across the room. The force of the impact pushed me back into the middle of the room where I started to pace in a circle trying to clear my head of the impact and the fury that raged inside. Questions of my existence filled my head as I pondered why I always got so angry. My eardrums begin throb with the sound of rushing water as the name of Jesus consumed my every thought. I fell to my knees, and I felt the presence and power of Jesus Christ. I began to ask for forgiveness and cried to Jesus to save me from my sins. My soul cried out for help as I realized that I couldn't do this on my own. It felt like I was on my knees for an hour confessing all my sins to God. As the burden of my sins got lighter as I cast them one by one onto Jesus, I began to feel the urge to forgive those who had hurt me. I knew

I needed to forgive just as God had forgiven me. As tears fell down my face, I asked God to help me forgive my dad for leaving me, to help me to forgive my mom, and to help me forgive the guy who sexually abused me. In that moment I laid all my burdens at the feet of Jesus Christ. My soul rejoiced as I was set free of the bandage of sin. In that moment, I was released from the hold that drugs, alcohol, sex, status, and power had on me. I could finally rest in the peace that surpasses all understanding.

"For whoever calls upon the name of the
LORD shall be saved." Romans 10:13

CHAPTER 15

FROM ONE SINNER TO ANOTHER

I want you to understand that God never intended for the world to be the way it is today. In Genesis, God saw His creation was good after each day, and it was perfect. Perfect until the first man and first woman disobeyed God, and things became chaotic. Satan tempted Eve and made the tree of knowledge of good and evil look pleasing, exciting, and desirable, just as sin looks today. God commanded Adam not to eat of the tree because he would surely die. Adam was standing behind Eve while Satan was twisting God's words. Adam was commanded to tend and protect the Garden in Eden, yet he allowed Satan to tempt his wife while standing next to her. They both ate of the tree, and complete chaos entered the world and they died spiritually, eventually dying physically. This is the reason the world is the way it is. Romans 3:23 says, "for all have sinned and fall short of the glory of God." Humanity is marred with sin at birth.

God wants you to understand He is holy and has nothing to do with sin, but God made a promise in Genesis 3:15 that the offspring of Eve would one day strike the head of Satan. Jesus fulfilled God's promise by suffering, dying, and rising from the grave. His perfect sacrifice was the only way to pay the penalty of sin. Finally, humanity could be reconciled with God. Adam and Eve were sent out of the presence of God and out of the Garden. Romans 6:23 says, "For the wages of sin is death, but God's gift is eternal life through Jesus Christ." God immediately had a plan because He loves humanity so much. He sacrificed His Son, Jesus Christ, to wash away the sins of the world. We do not deserve grace or mercy, but God freely gives it at the cost of "His only begotten Son" (John 3:16).

I want you to understand that God loves you, from one sinner to another. He loves you despite all the sins you have ever committed in your life. You will never be perfect, and you don't need to fix all your problems and sins before you come to Him because you will never be good enough or perfect enough to do that. He wants you to come as you are, repent from your sins, and put your hope and trust in Jesus Christ. Jesus says, "I Am the Way, the Truth, and the Life no one comes to the Father, but by Me" (John 14:6). You must confess to God you are a sinner and ask for forgiveness. You must understand and believe in your heart that Jesus died on the cross and rose from the grave. There is no other way unto salvation but through Christ and Christ alone.

"If you confess with your mouth the Lord Jesus and believe in your heart that God raised Him from the dead, you will be saved. One believes unto righteousness with the heart, and with the mouth, confession is made unto salvation." Romans 10:9-10

Whenever I was on my knees calling upon the name of Jesus, I prayed, "God help me, I have sinned against you, and I am asking for forgiveness. I believe that Jesus died on the cross and rose from the grave. Jesus, save me from my sins because I can't do this on my own, and I need you. My life is now yours, and I promise to walk the rest of my life serving you. Help me, Save me". I cried for a long time because I went through every sin I could ever remember. I began to count the cost of giving up my old way of life. I have been faithful almost every Sunday morning, Sunday evening, Wednesday evening service, and went to every revival I could make it to for the past eleven years. No one had to tell me I needed to be in church; I wanted to be in church because I knew I was changed and saved!